A TASTE OF
WEST AFRICA

Colin Harris

Thomson Learning
New York

Titles in this series

A TASTE OF

Britain	Italy
The Caribbean	Japan
China	Mexico
France	Spain
India	West Africa

Cover *A village in Dogon Territory, Mali.*

Title page *Young girls from Nigeria selling kola nuts.*

First published in the
United States in 1995 by
Thomson Learning
115 Fifth Avenue
New York, NY 10003

First published in Great Britain in 1994 by
Wayland (Publishers) Ltd.

Library of Congress Cataloging-in-Publication Data
Harris, Colin, 1937–
A taste of West Africa/ Colin Harris
p.   cm.—(Food around the world)
Includes bibliographical references and index.
ISBN 1-56847-185-8
1. Cookery, West African—Juvenile literature.
2. Food habits—Africa, West—Juvenile literature.
3. Africa, West—Social life and customs—Juvenile literature.
[1. Cookery, West African. 2. Food habits—Africa, West.
3. Africa, West—Social life and customs.] I. Title. II. Series.
TX725.W47H37   1994
641.5966—dc20   94-27119

Printed in Italy

Contents

The countries of West Africa

West Africa is a vast area of Africa, stretching over 1,500 miles from north to south and over 2,000 miles from east to west. The map on page 5 shows all the countries that make up West Africa. The Atlantic Ocean is a natural boundary to the south and west of the region. The northern boundary extends to the Sahara. In the east it is more difficult to tell where West Africa ends. The people of western Cameroon say they live in West Africa, but the Adamawa highlands, between Nigeria and Cameroon, are generally accepted as the eastern boundary.

A herd of cattle in the dry savanna of West Africa.

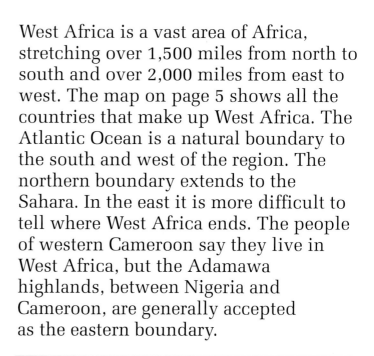

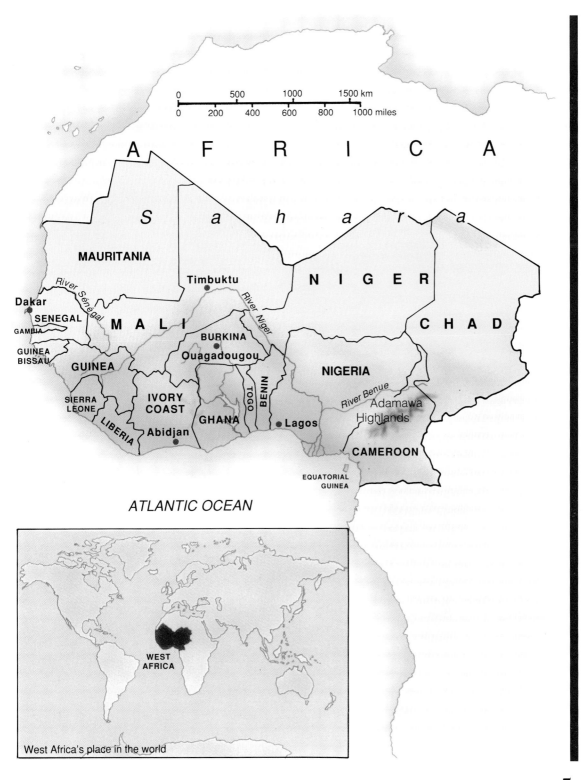

West Africa's place in the world

A taste of West Africa

Dakar, in Senegal, is one of the many large cities in West Africa.

A village in the southern rain forest of West Africa.

Most countries of West Africa have grassland with scattered trees, called the savanna. In the north, the savanna blends into dry *sahel* where few trees grow. But West Africa also has colorful rain forests, wide rivers, broad and shallow lakes, sandy beaches, and forested mountain slopes.

West Africa has a population of about 206 million. Many people live in such busy and exciting cities as Dakar and Lagos, or in romantic-sounding places such as Ouagadougou and Timbuktu, but most West Africans live in small villages.

History

Toward the end of the nineteenth century, Britain and France began to establish colonies in West Africa. At one time, every country in West Africa except Liberia was a British or French colony. Although all the former colonies are now independent countries, the

A shrine in Nigeria in honor of Oshun, an ancient goddess of the Yoruba people.

colonial powers have made a lasting impression on West Africa. They brought with them new ideas, including new foods and cooking methods, and they drew up the national boundaries that are still used today. European missionaries introduced Christianity to many West Africans.

Before the Europeans arrived in West Africa, there were several powerful and prosperous kingdoms. For example, the kingdom of Ghana flourished from the fourth to the eleventh century, when it was conquered by the Mali kingdom. The present-day countries of Ghana and Mali took their names from these ancient kingdoms. Other important kingdoms included the Songhai, the Yoruba, and the Benin kingdoms.

By the nineteenth century, Arabs from the Sahara region had introduced the Muslim religion to parts of West Africa.

Climate and vegetation

West Africa lies within the broad zone known as the tropics that circles the earth on each side of the equator. West Africa has a tropical climate. This means that, instead of hot and cold, the seasons are wet or dry. It is hot all year around, except on high mountains, but there are great differences in the amount of rain that falls and the kind of vegetation that grows.

The lush rain forests of the southern areas, where there is heavy rainfall.

Imagine a journey from Abidjan in Ivory Coast to Timbuktu in Mali. You would pass through three very different landscapes. At Abidjan on the southern coast, a long wet season is followed by a short dry season. There are lush rain forests where the branches of tall trees touch overhead like fingers. This layer of high branches is called "the canopy" because it forms a covering like a canopy, or tent, with no gaps in it. As you travel north, the wet season becomes shorter and the dry season becomes longer. The trees begin to thin out, and their branches no longer touch. Bushes and then grass grow between the trees. This is the beginning of the savanna. As you cross the savanna, trees

In northern, drier regions there is the savanna, where very few trees grow.

A taste of West Africa

Timbuktu is in the sahel *grasslands of Mali.*

become sparser and much shorter. They have thicker trunks to store water for the long dry season. By the time you have reached Timbuktu you are in the *sahel*, where there are very few trees and only clumps of grass. In the Sahara, there is no wet season at all.

Countries like Ghana, Benin, and Nigeria that stretch inland from the coast have more than one type of landscape and vegetation. Other countries, such as Mali, lie within the savanna or *sahel*.

Small trees are scattered across the dry sahel *in the northern regions of West Africa.*

Food in West Africa

Crops

In rural areas, most West Africans grow their own food on small plots of land near their villages. They first clear the land of trees and bushes and then plow the soil. When the rains come, they plant seeds. In dry years, when there is not enough rain for the crops, the harvest is poor.

A woman waters a vegetable plot near her village in Gambia.

A taste of West Africa

In the rain forest areas of West Africa, farmers clear the land and burn some of the vegetation so they can plant crops.

Cocoyams grow in a plot that has been cleared in the rain forest of southwest Cameroon.

The plot of land is used for one growing season only, then it is allowed to rest for several years. This is known as the fallow period, when the trees and bushes begin to grow again. Except in very dry seasons, this method of farming, called bush fallow, provides enough food for the people of West Africa. But as the population increases, farmers sometimes return to fallow plots too soon. If the soil has not had time to recover from the last crop, it is less fertile and the crops are not as healthy.

In the dry *sahel* region, lack of water can be a problem for farmers. The main crops here are millet and groundnuts, also known as peanuts or monkey nuts. Farmers of the forest and savannah areas have less difficulty growing food because the rains are more reliable. Here the main crops are cassava, cocoyams, and yams. These are all root crops, which

A young girl from Ghana feeds corn to the chickens. Most West African farmers have a few chickens or goats.

means they grow underground. Farmers also grow grain crops such as corn, millet, and guinea corn.

West African farmers also keep chickens and goats and grow vegetables and herbs. Women and men share the work, but the women usually do more farm work than the men.

13

Above *A boy has climbed a coconut tree to cut down a coconut.*

Below *Picking lemons on a plantation in Ivory Coast.*

Fruit

Root and grain crops are the staple, or main, foods in West Africa; however, the area also has a wide variety of fruits. Citrus fruits such as oranges, grapefruit, and lemons grow in the southern forest areas, and many people have citrus trees growing near their houses. West African oranges and grapefruits have green skins even when they are ripe. Bananas, plantains, and pineapples grow wild in the forests, but they are also grown on plantations. Coconut trees grow along the coast. Boys like to climb the trees and cut down the coconuts, which they enjoy for their refreshing milk and sweet nutty flesh. Pawpaws are easily grown in gardens in most parts of West Africa. Mangoes are common in the drier areas.

Right *A pineapple plantation.*

Farmers in the savanna raise cattle for meat and milk.

Cattle

Some farmers of the *sahel* region keep herds of cattle to be sold for meat. Thousands of cattle are herded across vast areas of the north. They frequently cross from one country to another in search of grass during the dry season. At one time the cattle traveled "on the hoof" to markets hundreds of miles away. Now they are more likely to be carried by road in trucks.

Fish

Fish are an important source of protein for West Africans. The wide Senegal, Niger, and Benue rivers provide a good supply of freshwater fish. Along the coast, fishermen go out in canoes and larger boats to catch fish from the Atlantic Ocean.

Before fish can be sent to inland markets, they are preserved. Women of

Fish caught off the coast of Senegal and left in the sun to dry.

Fishing in the swamps of Nigeria.

Women from northern Ghana sort the corn harvested from the fields near their village.

the coastal regions sometimes preserve fish in the traditional way by smoking them in ovens. But shops in the towns and cities also sell frozen fish that are either imported from outside West Africa or transported from coastal regions in boxes filled with ice or in refrigerated trucks.

Storing food

In the forest regions, vegetables, root crops, and grains are grown throughout most of the year, although crops grow better during the long wet season. Many foods, such as yams and corn, taste best when they are fresh, but they can also be stored for later. Food storage is particularly important in drier areas, where there may be long periods when there are no fresh crops.

Farmers must be very careful how they store their food. Insects and other animals that thrive in hot weather are serious pests. They eat crops growing in the field as well as food that has been harvested and stored. Each village or family compound has a large clay storage bin raised above the ground for protection against pests. When the harvest is good, the stored food lasts until the next harvest. But if the food is used up before then, people have to buy food from the market or go without. A food shortage can cause great hardship.

Storing millet in a Niger village.

A taste of West Africa

A woman pounds millet using a large mortar and pestle.

Grinding millet in a village in Burkina Faso. The building in the background is used to store grain.

Processing food

Corn, millet, and guinea corn are made into flour by pounding them with pestles in large wooden mortars. The flour, which is very coarse, is often made into porridge and cakes. Roots, such as cassava, are pressed and dried then pounded to make doughlike *fufu*, a very popular dish. *Fufu* can also be made from plantain, yams, and cocoyams. Wheat imported from North America and Europe is milled in factories to make flour for bread.

Foreign foods

Market stalls and shops sell foods from Europe and other parts of the world. Canned sardines and canned milk are particular favorites. French foods such as croissants and baguettes can be found in countries such as Togo and Senegal that were once French colonies. An English breakfast of bacon and eggs is part of the menu in big hotels in former British colonies such as Nigeria and Ghana.

Above *Baguettes are popular in countries that were once French colonies.*
Below *This grocery stall is selling many imported items.*

Village life

Many West African homes have corrugated metal roofs rather than traditional thatch roofs.

Homes

The traditional West African house was built of sun-dried bricks or mud with a thatched roof made of grass. Many homes these days, even in rural areas, are made from cinder blocks and have corrugated metal roofs. Villages that are near towns may have an electricity supply, but in more isolated places homes have no electricity. In the past, villagers fetched water from a well that was shared by everyone. Today, villagers still have to fetch their own water, but

Standpipes pump water from a village well in Gambia.

most villages have a standpipe that pumps water from the well. In dry areas, there may be no village well, and water must be fetched from a nearby river.

In villages throughout West Africa, women have traditionally cooked in clay pots on open wood fires or on charcoal stoves made of sheet metal. Gradually, the clay cooking pots are being replaced with aluminum pots and pans.

Food

Villagers eat the food they grow themselves, which sometimes means there is not much variety. People often eat the same thing for every meal. Any extra food is sold at the local market or, if the village is near a main road, it is sold to passing travelers. At the market, villagers can buy other types of food that are not grown locally, perhaps even imported foods such as canned milk.

Villagers often sell their extra food to passing travelers.

A taste of West Africa

Early morning is the coolest time of day, so everyone gets up very early. A typical breakfast would be corn porridge, fruit, bread, and tea. But for children who have a long distance to go to school, there may not be time for much breakfast. Children usually take their lunches with them, but if the school is nearby they come home for lunch. In the evening, when the whole family is together, the main meal of the day is eaten. Food is eaten with fingers, and usually served in bowls rather than on plates.

A family in Senegal enjoys a meal in the open air.

City life

Every West African country has modern cities, with traffic-filled streets, public buildings, parks, hotels, and department stores. More and more West Africans are leaving the villages and moving to the towns and cities in search of work. In Nigeria and Cameroon, there will soon be more people living in towns than in villages. City life can be exciting; there are markets, restaurants, entertainment, and new people to meet.

The city of Lagos is on the coast of Nigeria.

But many who arrive in the city cannot find jobs, so they have to move in with relatives and rely on them to help them survive in the city.

Homes

Every city and town has large apartment buildings and solid concrete houses. These homes have running water and electricity. Food is cooked on electric or propane stoves.

But many people cannot afford such luxuries and have to live in smaller, less comfortable houses. Often these houses have no running water, and neighbors have to share standpipes in the street.

Food

People living in towns and cities generally eat the same types of food as the villagers, but there is a greater selection of food to choose from in the markets and stores. Open-air

This woman is preparing banku, *a dish made with cassava or corn. Many people in the towns and cities of West Africa have gas or electric stoves, but they still follow the traditional recipes and methods of cooking.*

markets sell a wide variety of fresh fruit, vegetables, grains, meat, and fish. In the cities and large towns, there are imported and frozen foods for sale at supermarkets and "cold stores." A cold store is a shop with a frozen food section that contains either imported or locally produced frozen food.

Eating out is not a problem in towns and cities. Street traders sell bread, roasted groundnuts, fresh sliced fruit, and cooked snacks. There are also small restaurants known as "chop bars" that offer cooked meals, snacks, and drinks.

Supermarkets sell a variety of imported foods.

West African dishes

Cassava, a root vegetable, is used in many West African dishes.

Crushed cassava being rolled into small balls.

Starchy root vegetables, such as cassava or yams, are part of most West African dishes. The vegetables are usually boiled and served with meat or fish. Boiled yams are delicious when served with fish fried in oil and ginger. Mashed cooked yams are sometimes mixed with eggs and fried as yam balls. These are eaten plain or mixed with slices of tomatoes and sweet red peppers.

Almost every West African home has a *fufu* pounder, which is like a large mortar and pestle. Pieces of cooked yam, cassava, cocoyam, or plantain are crushed in the mortar and then pounded with water until a soft lump of *fufu* is formed. The pounding is usually done outside the house. *Fufu* with pepper soup is a typical meal. Pieces of *fufu* are broken off and eaten with the fingers.

Chicken is a favorite meat in stews and soups. Locally grown vegetables and herbs may be added for extra flavor. Groundnut stew, made with chicken, crushed groundnuts, tomatoes, onions, and peppers, is popular. So is the much spicier pepper chicken stew. These dishes are served with boiled rice, yams, sweet potatoes, or plantains.

A rich oily stew made from palm oil is a good source of vitamin B. The palm oil produces a thick orange layer on top of the stew.

Rice, which grows only in the wetter regions, is rather expensive to buy, so it is usually saved for special occasions. One party dish that is popular throughout West Africa is *Jollof* rice.

West Indian cooking

Many West African dishes are also enjoyed in the West Indies. For well over a hundred years, West Africans were taken as slaves to the West Indies, where their recipes and their cooking traditions were passed on.

Left *Palm oil for sale at a market in Togo.*

Below *Oil palm fruit.*

A taste of West Africa

This spicy Jollof *rice and fish dish is often served on special occasions.*

Jollof rice is a mixture of rice, tomatoes, onions, pepper, and spices boiled together and served with a choice of fried chicken, beef, or goat. This recipe comes from Senegal where it is the national dish of the Wolof people.

Kiliwili (also spelled *Kelewele*) is a popular snack, often sold at roadside stands. Pieces of plantain are coated with cayenne pepper and fried in oil. It is very spicy!

West Africans eat few cooked desserts. A choice of fresh fruit is usually eaten after the main course. A favorite treat for children is to chew on a piece of sugarcane, which grows in the forest area of West Africa.

To be fit and healthy, West African children, like children everywhere, need a balanced diet that includes a variety of energy foods, proteins, vitamins, and minerals. Children are taught at school what foods to eat in order to stay healthy.

Unfortunately, some people, especially in the drier northern regions, do not always get enough of certain foods and, therefore, may be undernourished. But this happens less frequently in the south where fresh fruits and vegetables are plentiful throughout the year.

Above *A girl sells mangoes in Burkina Faso. In most southern countries of West Africa, fresh fruits and vegetables are usually available.*

Left *This man and woman are preparing* garri, *which is pounded cassava fried in palm oil.*

Feasts

Religious festivals, weddings, funerals, and other special events are times for feasts. One particularly exciting and colorful celebration is the "enstoolment" of a new chief. The chief's stool, or throne, is a specially carved seat on which he is proclaimed ruler of the people. His queen's stool is similar but slightly smaller. On these occasions, the chief and other village elders wear traditional clothes, and there is drumming, dancing, and feasting.

West Africans enjoy lots of different celebrations and festivals that include music, dancing, and special food.

For Christians, Christmas and Easter are also times for feasts. The Muslims of West Africa celebrate the end of Ramadan – the month of daytime fasting and prayer – with a special feast.

A typical festive meal is *Jollof* rice and goat meat. Usually the adults drink palm wine. This is made from the sap of certain palm trees. When the palm wine is fresh and sweet, children are allowed to drink it. But after a few days, the wine becomes too strong for children.

In some parts of the south, there is a yam festival when the yams are harvested. This is a good time to have a feast of fresh yams.

These dancers at a festival in Mali are wearing traditional costumes and masks.

Porridge

This porridge is made from millet. It looks like, but does not taste like, hot oatmeal.

Ingredients
Serves 4

1 cup millet
1¾ cups water
salt
sugar

Equipment

saucepan
wooden spoon
small serving
 bowls

Harvested millet tied in bundles.

1 Put the water in the saucepan with a little salt and bring to a boil. Add the millet.

Always be careful with boiling liquid. Ask an adult to help you.

2 Cook until soft, stirring constantly.

3 Serve in bowls and sprinkle with sugar.

Fruit salad

Fruit for sale in Abidjan, Ivory Coast.

Ingredients
Serves 6–8

½ pineapple
1 pawpaw (if
   available)
1 mango
2 bananas
½ coconut or
   shredded
   coconut
2 oranges
2 tbls. lemon juice
1 lime cut into
   wedges

Equipment

knife
chopping board
large mixing bowl
wooden spoon
serving bowls

1 Cut the pineapple into rings or wedges. Peel and slice the other fruits (except the lime).

Always be careful when using a knife. Ask an adult to help you.

2 Mix all the fruit together with the lemon juice in a large bowl. Serve in smaller bowls with a wedge of lime to squeeze over the salad.

Kiliwili

Ingredients
Serves 4–6

2 plantains or
   unripe
   bananas
1 tablespoon
   cayenne
   pepper or
   paprika
2–3 tablespoons
   peanut or corn
   oil

Equipment

knife
chopping board
bowl for
   cayenne or
   paprika
frying pan
tongs or spatula
paper towel

Plantains are used to make kiliwili.

1 Peel the plantains or bananas and cut them into bite-sized pieces.

3 Heat the oil in the frying pan and fry the plantain or banana pieces slowly until they are brown and crispy on the outside.

2 Dip the pieces gently in cayenne pepper or paprika. Shake off any loose cayenne pepper. It can be very spicy!

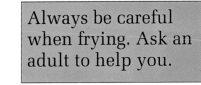

Always be careful when frying. Ask an adult to help you.

Be very careful when using cayenne pepper. It can irritate your skin, mouth, eyes, nose, or any part of the body it touches.

4 Using the tongs, remove the pieces from the frying pan and drain on pieces of paper towel.

5 Serve while still warm.

Groundnut stew

Ingredients
Serves 8

3 pounds of boneless
   chicken, cut in
   pieces
small onion, chopped
½ teaspoon salt
1 tablespoon crunchy
peanut butter

water
1 tablespoon tomato
   puree
1 teaspoon cayenne
   pepper

Equipment

saucepan
wooden spoon

36

Always be careful with boiling liquid. Ask an adult to help you.

1 Put the chicken pieces, salt, and onion in the saucepan and cover with water. Cook for about 30 minutes.

2 Add more water if necessary to cover the chicken.

3 Add the tomato puree and cayenne pepper and stir. Cook for 20 minutes.

4 Add the peanut butter and stir. Simmer for 10 minutes.

5 Serve with fluffy white rice or yams and boiled plantains.

Fufu

Ingredients
Serves 4

2 yams,
    plantains, or
    unripe
    bananas
water
hot water as
    needed for
    mixing

Equipment

saucepan
large mortar and
    pestle
serving bowls

This woman is making fufu.

1 Peel the yams, plantains, or unripe bananas and cut into pieces. Boil in water until soft.

Always be careful with boiling liquid. Ask an adult to help you.

2 Put the pieces into the mortar, one by one, and pound carefully.

3 Add small amounts of hot water as needed to keep the mixture moist. Keep pounding and adding water until the *fufu* sticks together in one lump.

4 Divide the *fufu* into small balls and place in the serving bowls. Serve with soup or vegetables.

Jollof *rice*

Planting seedlings in a rice field in Sierra Leone. Rice is grown only in the wetter areas, but it is eaten throughout West Africa.

1 Put the rice and water into the saucepan and bring to a boil. Turn the heat down and simmer for 8 minutes.

Always be careful with boiling liquid. Ask an adult to help you.

2 The rice will be partly cooked. Mix in the tomato puree, onions, cayenne pepper, mixed herbs, thyme, butter, black pepper, white pepper, and salt.

3 Continue to simmer until the rice is almost cooked. Add the tomatoes.

4 When the rice is done, add warm pieces of cooked chicken and mix together. Serve in a large bowl.

Ingredients
Serves 6–8

2 cups white rice
1 quart water
½ cup tomato puree
1 large onion, sliced
1 teaspoon cayenne
 pepper
1 tablespoon mixed
 herbs
sprig of thyme
5 tablespoons butter
black and white
 pepper to taste
salt to taste
2 large tomatoes,
 peeled and sliced
1 pound fried or
 stewed chicken, cut
 into pieces

Equipment

large saucepan
knife
chopping board
wooden spoon
serving bowl

Ginger fried fish

Ingredients

Serves 4

2 pounds of rock
   eel (or any firm
   white fish,
   such as
   haddock)
½ tablespoon
   ground ginger
1 onion, chopped
   fine
½ teaspoon
   cayenne
   pepper
salt to taste
2 tablespoons
   peanut or
   corn oil
parsley sprigs

Equipment

large bowl
knife
chopping board
frying pan
spatula

A fish catch on the coast of Gambia.

Ginger fried fish

1 Cut the fish into small pieces.

Always be careful when frying. Ask an adult to help you.

3 Fry the fish in oil. Turn to fry on all sides.

2 Place fish in a bowl with ground ginger, onion, cayenne pepper, and salt. Stir. Let stand for 15 minutes.

4 Serve with sprigs of parsley. This dish goes well with boiled yams or rice.

Pawpaw and lime

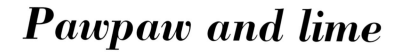

1 Cut the pawpaw into four wedges and scoop out the black seeds.

2 Serve each wedge in a bowl with a slice of lime on top.

Always be careful when using a knife. Ask an adult to help you.

3 Squeeze the lime onto the pawpaw just before eating.

Glossary

Cassava A root vegetable, shaped like a carrot, with brown skin and white flesh.

Christian A follower of Christianity, the religion based on the teachings of Jesus Christ.

Cinder blocks Lightweight building blocks made from sand and cement mixed with coal cinders.

Citrus fruit A type of slightly acid fruit covered with thick skin that grows on trees or shrubs in tropical climates. Oranges, lemons, limes, and grapefruit are all citrus fruits.

Cocoyam A root vegetable. A cocoyam is smaller than a yam and looks a little like a cassava.

Colony A region that is ruled by people from another country.

Compound A group of houses in an enclosed space with a shared front yard and garden. A large, extended family of mother, father, children, aunts, uncles, grandparents, and cousins may live together in one family compound.

Corrugated Formed into folds and grooves.

Diet The foods a person normally eats.

Equator An imaginary line that circles the middle of the earth.

Fallow When referring to land, fallow means leaving it unused for one or more growing seasons in order to make the soil more fertile.

Fertile When referring to soil, fertile means very rich and nourishing, thus encouraging plant growth.

Grassland Land where grass is the main form of plant life.

Groundnut A type of underground bean, such as a peanut, with two kernels that grow in a pod or shell.

Guinea corn A type of grain similar to millet that is used to make porridge or is ground into flour.

Harvest The fruit, vegetables, or grains that are picked at the end of the growing season.

Imported Brought into the country from another country.

Isolated Far from any other village or town.

Millet A pale yellow grain that grows well in dry climates.

Minerals Substances such as iron and zinc that are found in certain foods in small amounts and are necessary for a healthy diet.

Missionaries People sent by a religious organization (usually the Christian church) to a foreign country to work with people there and to teach the people their religion.

Mortar A very hard bowl in which substances are ground or pounded with a pestle.

Muslim A follower of the religion called Islam and the teachings of the Prophet Mohammed.

Pestle A club-shaped tool used to pound or grind herbs or grains in a mortar.

Plantain A starchy tropical fruit similar to a banana. Plantains are treated as vegetables rather than fruit and are fried, baked, or dried and ground into flour.

Plantation A large area of land used to grow a single crop, such as pineapples.

Processing When referring to food, processing means treating in such a way that the food lasts longer or can be used more easily.

Protein The main bodybuilding substance found in certain foods.

Ramadan A month when Muslims say extra prayers, give money to the poor, and fast during the day.

Rural Of the countryside.

Sahel A region of dry savanna south of the Sahara.

Savanna Grassland with few trees.

Traditional According to tradition, which is a way of doing something that has not changed for years.

Tropical Having to do with the tropics, the area around the equator that is hot all year long.

Undernourished Not receiving all the vitamins, minerals, and proteins needed to stay healthy.

Vitamins Substances found in foods in tiny amounts. Vitamins are necessary for normal growth and general health.

Yam A root vegetable with brownish pink skin and white flesh. It is similiar to, but not the same as, a sweet potato.

Further information

Recipe Books

Kenda, Margaret and Williams, Phyllis S. *Cooking Wizardry for Kids*. Barron, 1990.

Nabwire, Constance and Montgomery, Bertha Vining. *Cooking the African Way*. Easy Menu Ethnic Cookbooks. Minneapolis: Lerner Publications, 1988.

Wilkes, Angela. *My First Cookbook*. New York: Alfred A. Knopf Books for Young Readers, 1989.

Information Books

Achu, Kamala. *Nigeria*. Countries of the World. New York: Bookwright Press, 1992.

Hintz, Martin. *Ghana*. Rev. ed. Enchantment of the World. Chicago: Childrens Press, 1992.

Lerner Geography Department. *Mali in Pictures*. Visual Geography Series. Minneapolis: Lerner Publications, 1990.

Wilkins, Frances. *Gambia*. Places and Peoples of the World. New York: Chelsea House, 1988.

Picture acknowledgments

The publishers would like to thank the following for allowing their photographs to be reproduced: Anthony Blake Photo Library 44 (K. Kleineman); Chapel Studios: Zul *cover* inset, 20 top (Nicola Swainson); Christine Osborne Pictures 9, 20 bottom, 21, 25, 26 bottom, 28, 36; Eye Ubiquitous 6 top, 27 left (Thelma Sanders), 34 (Trip), 42; Panos Pictures, 10 top (David Reed), 11 (Trygve Bolstad), 14 top (Penny Tweedie), 14 bottom left and right (Ron Giling), 15 both (Jeremy Hartley), 16 both (Bruce Paton), 17 (Ron Giling), 18 bottom (Jeremy Hartley), 19 top (Ron Giling), 22 (Jeremy Hartley), 29 top (Ron Giling), 32 (Rex Parry), 33 (Ron Giling), 40 (Jeremy Hartley); Edward Parker 4, 6 bottom, 10 bottom, 12 bottom, 12 top (P. E. Parker), 27 right (P. E. Parker), 31; Tony Stone Worldwide *cover;* Tropix 13 (M. & V. Birley), 19 bottom (M. & V. Birley), 24 (M. & V. Birley), 26 top (D. Parker), 38 (M. & V. Birley); Wayland Picture Library *title page,* 7, 8, 23, 29 bottom, 30 (all by James Morris).

The map artwork on page 5 was supplied by Peter Bull. The recipe artwork on pages 32 to 44 was supplied by Judy Stevens.

Index

48